Between Nothingness And Eternity

Sri Chinmoy

Ganapati Press

© 2024 SRI CHINMOY CENTRE

ISBN 978-1-911319-59-7

First edition: Published 1982
Reprint: 11 October 2024

Ganapati Press.
29 Campbell Road, Oxford, OX4 3PF
www.ganapatipress.org

Contents

Between Nothingness and Eternity	13
Where is the Truth?	14
Immortality	15
In Secrecy Supreme	16
The Swing of Delight	17
I Sing Because You Sing	18
The Wave	19
The Eye of my Eye	20
The Slaves of Fate	21
Inside Emptiness	22
Journey	23
In Atom and in Pollen	24
Silence of Infinity	25
The Eternal Seeker	26
Beyond Speech and Mind	27
The Eternal Presence	28
Pretence No More	29
Silence-Face, Forgiveness-Smile	30
Nothing Happened	31
I Do the Impossible	32
Ultimately Everything Becomes Boring	33
Eternal Warrior	34
A Symbol of Promise	35
The Supreme (1)	36

The Supreme (2)	37
Believe Me	38
Selves	39
Mystery	40
The Collector	41
Play	42
Love is This, Love is That	43
Darkness	44
Birthmark	45
Songs of Passing Time	46
When They Knock at Your Door	47
The Waters of Peace	48
The Forest of My Heart	49
The Message of Surrender	50
A Speck of Dust	51
Only One Hope	52
How Many Songs?	53
I Long to be One	54
Be Thou	55
Apocalypse	56
Revelation	57
Farewell Time	58
My Life's Last Game	59
Father-Son	60
Ever the Same Again	61
The Absolute	62

INTRODUCTION

Poetry as Mantra

When a poet addresses himself to the expression of the highest spiritual truth, what Aldous Huxley called "expressing the inexpressible," he must necessarily face the paradox inherent in such an undertaking. In other words, he knows that what he is trying to articulate is beyond the scope of language, and yet the attempt must be made, the demand will not be denied. For nothing else, ultimately, is worth expressing.

Knowing that what he has to say might be better communicated by music, or, even more directly, in the profound silence of meditation, he has to find a mode which can do justice to the intensity of his vision.

Sri Chinmoy, the Indian poet and mystic, has evolved such a mode, and he has done so, moreover, in English, a language less fluid, less musical, than his native Bengali.

As an Indian writing in English, he is heir, as it were, to two separate traditions. There are affinities, for example, with Herbert and Blake, with Hopkins and Whitman. Yet there are respects in which he has gone beyond any of these, and for a fuller understanding of his achievement it is necessary to look at the Indian background to his writing.

There are two Sanskrit terms which are particularly important in understanding his poetry – *mantra* and *sutra*.

Many in the West will be familiar with the idea of *mantra* in relation to the practice of meditation. A *mantra* is in its simplest form a syllable or set of syllables, chanted aloud as an aid to meditation. There is an awareness here of the power of the word as incantation, invocation. Poetry described as mantric actually *invokes* the qualities it describes.

Nolini Kanta Gupta, a contemporary Indian poet and philosopher, has written, "The highest form and the most perfect perfection of poetry lie in the mantra." In mantric poetry, he suggests, "speech is not the dress or outer garb of an experience, but the realization of an inner delight."

He quotes as examples the writings of the great *rishis*, the seer-poets of India, who composed the *Vedas*, the *Upanishads*, the *Gita*. (It is interesting that Eliot chose to end *The Waste Land* with a mantric invocation of peace – *Shantih Shantih Shantih* – quoted from the Upanishads, clearly recognizing the power and resonance of these ancient modes.)

The word *sutra* may be less familiar to Western readers. Literally it means thread, and it is used to describe series of terse, aphoristic utterances, perhaps the best known being the Yoga Sutras of Patanjali. These offer instruction in the path of

Yoga, and are tight, densely packed, designed to be memorized and recited aloud, gradually unfolding their truth.

Many of Sri Chinmoy's short poems are also instructional, their apparent simplicity revealing more and more profound depth on each re-reading. They display a haiku-like compactness, a tremendous density and compression of language.

He has, in fact, forged his own language, his own vocabulary, imbued familiar words with a new life, an energy and vitality. His style is unique, instantly recognizable.

It is a style at once lyrical and abstract – there are few *things* in his poems, and those that do appear are surcharged with meaning: they are archetypes, images that function as symbols – bird, boat, tree, flower, flame. He is above all a poet of the *inner* landscape, and he never forgets that the poem is "a finger pointing at the moon," an invitation to the silence beyond the words.

It is a poetry which, for all its simplicity, can be difficult, demanding, though not in the usual sense of these terms, where the demand is on the intellect, struggling to unravel something obscure. Rather what is demanded here is a qualitative leap of consciousness; the reader has to *come up* to the level of the poems. There has to be an active participation. The understanding has to be *experiential*. "A poem should not mean / but be" wrote Archibald McLeish. And a poem exists, has its being, not flat on the page, but in its total effect.

Some years ago Scottish poet Tom McGrath was reading one of Sri Chinmoy's poems to another writer, using the poems, as it happens, to illustrate the impossibility of expressing in English what he regarded as a peculiarly Indian sensibility. Tom thought the particular poem was in some way "old-fashioned" in its rhythm, in its diction. But somehow he realized he was not making his point. What happened as he read the poem, he describes as follows – "The words sprang from my lips and sounded in the room with an authority that was awe-inspiring. It became clear that we were listening to a voice speaking from the absolute pinnacle of human experience, and speaking directly from it. By the time we reached the closing lines, we were both dumbfounded. Not only had we heard a great poem, but we both felt we had been in the presence of a consciousness the nature of which filled us with the deepest humility and reverence. Thereafter, I had a new respect for Sri Chinmoy's poetry..."

The poem in question was *The Absolute*, which is included in this volume. It is one of the poems in which Sri Chinmoy is most clearly working in what I have called the "mantric" mode.

And the tone of authority is unmistakable. To put it quite simply, he *knows*. He does not have to argue his case, he just states it. This can be a disconcerting experience for the reader unused to such certainty of tone. I am reminded of Christopher Isherwood's description of the language spoken by Krishna in the *Bhagavad Gita* – "like a University lecture delivered by God!"

From what I have said, it will be clear that the poems are intended to be read aloud. (To hear Sri Chinmoy recite them is a moving and uplifting experience.) He has, in fact, set many of his poems to music, enhancing them, adding another dimension. He is fond of quoting his great compatriot Tagore –

> "To the birds you gave songs, the birds gave you songs in return.
> You gave me only a voice, yet asked for more, and I sing."

It is this *more* that he pours out into these poems, songs, mantras, and it speaks directly to what Yeats called "the deep heart's core." Their simplicity is often deceptive, like water so clear it belies its depth. It is a simplicity that is hard won, the ultimate resolution of all complexity.

In contemporary literature he is, I believe, unique. There is nothing really to compare with his achievement, because there is no one writing from the same level of *inner* accomplishment, the same perspective.

If I have tried to "place" Sri Chinmoy's writing, it

is not with the intention of limiting it, of consigning it to a category. In fact I think he has created his own space, his own category, beyond the ebb and flow of literary fashion.

Alan Spence.

Alan Spence is an award-winning poet and playwright, novelist and short story writer. He is Professor Emeritus in Creative Writing at the University of Aberdeen.

BETWEEN NOTHINGNESS
AND ETERNITY

BETWEEN NOTHINGNESS AND ETERNITY

Barren of events,
Rich in pretensions
My earthly life.

Obscurity
My real name.

Wholly unto myself
I exist.

I wrap no soul
In my embrace.

No mentor worthy
Of my calibre
Have I.

I am all alone
Between failure and frustration.

I am the red thread
Between Nothingness
And Eternity.

WHERE IS THE TRUTH?

O Lord, where is the Truth?
  "Where your Beloved is."
Who is my Beloved, Who?
  "In Whom your life is peace."

IMMORTALITY

I feel in all my limbs His boundless Grace;
Within my heart the Truth of life shines white.
The secret heights of God my soul now climbs;
No dole, no sombre pang, no death in my sight.

No mortal days and nights can shake my calm;
A Light above sustains my secret soul.
All doubts with grief are banished from my deeps,
My eyes of light perceive my cherished Goal.

Though in the world, I am above its woe;
I dwell in an ocean of supreme release.
My mind, a core of the One's unmeasured thoughts,
The star-vast welkin hugs my Spirit's peace.

My eternal days are found in speeding time;
I play upon His Flute of rhapsody.
Impossible deeds no more impossible seem;
In birth-chains now shines Immortality.

IN SECRECY SUPREME

In secrecy supreme I see You.
You live in my eyes, in my sleep,
In my dreams, in my sweet wakefulness.
In the stupendous mirth of life,
In the abysmal lap of death,
You I behold.
Your Love-Play is my world.

THE SWING OF DELIGHT

Hope-river flows, hope-river flows.
In the lap of the unknown
Is the river of smile.
At every moment I cry and weep with hope;
Again it is I who dance with my Lord
In the swing of delight.

I SING BECAUSE YOU SING

I sing because You sing.
I smile because You smile.
Because You play on the flute
I have become Your flute.
You play in the depths of my heart.
You are mine, I am Yours.
This is my sole identification.
In one Form You are my Mother and Father eternal,
And Consciousness-moon, Consciousness-sun
  all-pervading.

THE WAVE

The wave subsides and the wave rises.
The flower withers and the flower blossoms.
There is no end to human wants
And human achievements.
Nothing is permanent and nothing is fleeting.
Then for whom shall we cry,
For what shall we cry?
Whom shall we invoke
With a new thought and new form?
Everything eventually blossoms.

THE EYE OF MY EYE

By whose touch does the lily smile
And open its beauty-bud?
Whose beauty's moonlight
Do I see in the lily?
Who is the Eye of my eye?
Who is the Heart of my heart?
Alas, why do I not see Him,
His Face of transcendental Beauty,
Even in my dreams?

THE SLAVES OF FATE

In the universal heart all hearts are one,
  inseparable, I know.
Yet knowing this, I hurt the hearts of others
  day and night.
We are all the slaves of fate;
It dances on our foreheads.
In peace sublime is the extinction-sleep of fate.
I know this secret.
O Jewel of my eye, pour into my heart Your
  golden Silence.

INSIDE EMPTINESS

Inside emptiness
Fullness abides.
And inside fullness
The bondage of the finite
Is totally smashed.
Once we are there
We hear the supreme Victory
Of the Absolute Supreme.

JOURNEY

I journeyed into time,
I journeyed into space,
I journeyed into skies,
I failed to see His Face.

IN ATOM AND IN POLLEN

In atom and in pollen
And in human frames
My life abides.
All beauty am I,
Immutable am I.
I drink my ambrosia
All alone.

SILENCE OF INFINITY

My world is for Your Feet.
My life is for Your Dream.
O Silence of Infinity,
O Immortality of Heaven,
Come, come, come,
This heart remains ever awake.

THE ETERNAL SEEKER

I know, I know,
It is I who have to discover myself.
I am the eternal seeker of my own reality.
Here on earth I shall have to discover everything.
Here in the finite I have to see You,
O my Reality's Form,
O Infinity and Infinity's Immortal Life.

BEYOND SPEECH AND MIND

Beyond speech and mind,
Into the river of ever-effulgent Light
My heart dives.
Today thousands of doors, closed for millennia,
Are opened wide.

THE ETERNAL PRESENCE

There was a time when I loved
The fantastic fabrics of the mind.
There was a time
When I lived my life
Based on culled fictions.
There was a time
When I was satisfied
With a fragment of reality,
Splintered, broken and smashed.
But now a lucid illumination
Steals into my heart.
The eternal Presence
Of Infinity's Light
Feeds my Vision's Dawn.

PRETENCE NO MORE

I live in a zone of silence
To decipher my hostile past.
No, my life is not
A speck of dust
Flawed and doomed to nothingness.
Useless words I pronounced.
Therefore suicide I committed
Time and again.
In my life from now on
    Only
The essential is permissible.
No more shall I pretend to be
What I am not:
    Ignorance.

SILENCE-FACE, FORGIVENESS-SMILE

Life is but a day.
    Therefore
I try to finish
    All my aspiring
      And
    All my loving
In the short span
    Of one single day.

Life is but Eternity,
    Therefore
I sleep and dream,
    I sing and dance
      And
    Dance and sing
In the Silence-Face, Forgiveness-Smile
    Of the birthless and deathless Day.

NOTHING HAPPENED

Nothing really exciting happened
When I fell down from Heaven.
I just fell down.

Nothing really exciting happened
When I climbed up to the skies.
I just climbed up.

Nothing really exciting happened
When I starved with darkness.
I just starved.

Nothing really exciting happened
When I dined with Light.
I just dined.

I DO THE IMPOSSIBLE?

I have decided what I want.
I shall listen to the voice within.
I believe
It is all-loving, all-fulfilling.
I know
It is all-loving, all-fulfilling.
And it is exactly so.
My belief is my power.
My knowledge is my power.
I do the impossible because
My life of constant surrender
To the Will of the Supreme
Has taught me how.

ULTIMATELY EVERYTHING BECOMES BORING

Ultimately everything
    Becomes boring.
Even great miracles
    Become boring.
Even the tremendous powers of the cosmic gods
    Become boring.
Even God the Omniscient
    Becomes boring.
Even God the Omnipotent
    Becomes boring.
    But, but, but
God the All-Love
    Never becomes boring.
      Never.

ETERNAL WARRIOR

You have given me eyes,
But You have not given me sight.
You have given me a heart,
But You have not given me love.
Around me is the hope of the false city.
In this life-game, whichever road I walk along,
In the twinkling of an eye that road is closed.
I am the eternal warrior; I am the eternal war.

A SYMBOL OF PROMISE

Every life is a rich
    Storehouse
Of experience.
I dare declare:
We live not,
    NOT
In an epoch of
Chaotic decay.
I plumb the depths
    Of light
At each hush-gap.

Every life
Is a symbol of
    Promise,
Streaming forth from a realm
    Where
No one is a stranger, unwanted
    None,
Where Love blossoms for the One
And Truth for the many.

THE SUPREME (1)

Father, I have seen.
    "No."
Father, I have known.
    "No."
Father, I have felt.
    "No."
Father, I have become.
    "No."
Father, I AM.
    "Yes."

THE SUPREME (2)

Father, You are the Grace.
    "No."
Father, You are the Law.
    "No."
Father, You are the Birth
    and
      Death of Creation.
    "No."
Father, You are the Child
    of
      Your DREAM.
    "Yes."

BELIEVE ME

I have seen the black wings of death.
Believe me, I was not frightened.

I have seen the white wings of Heaven.
Believe me, I was not elated.

I have seen the red wings of earth.
Believe me, I am really concerned.

SELVES

We see
Only what we are.
We are
Our skin-deep selves.
We are
Our dissatisfied million selves.
We are
Our eyeless emotion-selves.
We are
Our helpless frustration-selves.
We are
Reaping the full harvest of our forgotten selves.

MYSTERY

Whatever appears to leave us
Actually does not leave us.
Whatever appears to stay with us
Actually does not stay.
Everything is a mystery
Of constant gain and loss.

THE COLLECTOR

I collect fame,
The dust of time.

I collect pride,
The foot of time.

I collect truth,
The pride of time.

I collect love,
The life of time.

PLAY

I shall play with everyone
On the day I play with You.
I shall blend in every heart
On the day I blend in You.

LOVE IS THIS, LOVE IS THAT

Love is the road that leads
Our souls to union vast.
Love is the passion-storm
That sports with our vital dust.

Love's child is emotion-flame.
Love's eyes are freedom, fear.
Love's heart is breath or death.
And love is cheap, love dear.

DARKNESS

The darkness of night,
The darkness of dawn,
The darkness of day,
The darkness of light,
The darkness of the sun:
All these he became,

Only to transcend the unreal in himself,
Feel the reality in himself,
And become the eternal in himself.

BIRTHMARK

Some are born with aspiration-seed.
I am born with desire-tree.

Some are born with realisation-flower.
I am born with suspicion-fruit.

SONGS OF PASSING TIME

Childhood sings
The songs of strange curiosity.

Adolescence sings
The songs of blind carelessness.

Youth sings
The songs of cold indifference.

Maturity sings
The songs of deepening nostalgia.

Dotage sings
The songs of orphan helplessness.

WHEN THEY KNOCK AT YOUR DOOR

    When
Animal the child
Knocks at your door,
Feed him with your wisdom.
       He is hungry.

    When
Man the child
Knocks at your door,
Bless him with your power.
       He is weak.

    When
God the child
Knocks at your door,
Embrace Him with your love.
       He is lonely.

THE WATERS OF PEACE

In how many ways You have sung
The song of liberation in my heart.
In return You have received only unbearable pain.
I see all around me the heavy load of poverty
And the slumber of inconscience.
How can I lose myself in the waters of peace?

THE FOREST OF MY HEART

I shall now call myself;
I shall now call.
In the forest of my heart, seeing myself,
I shall love myself and love myself.
I shall be my own quest,
My absolute wealth.
The journey of light supreme will commence
In the heart of freedom.

THE MESSAGE OF SURRENDER

Today You have given me
The message of surrender.
I have offered to You
My very flower-heart.
In the dark night with tears,
In the unknown prison-cell of illusion,
In the house of the finite,
No longer shall I abide.
I know You are mine.
I have known this, Mother,
O Queen of the Eternal.

A SPECK OF DUST

I know, I am a speck of dust.
Yet the Mother of the Universe
Eternally stays with me.
She is my Eternal Companion.
She is my only Consolation.
On the one hand, I am the poorest of all.
On the other hand, I am the child of light
Of the Mother of the Universe.
May I remain unperturbed
In all happiness and sorrows.

ONLY ONE HOPE

Break asunder all my hopes.
Only keep one hope,
And that hope is to learn
The language of Your inner Silence
In my utter unconditional surrender.
In Your clear and free sky
I shall be calm and perfect.
The bird of my heart is dancing today
In the festival of supernal Light.

HOW MANY SONGS

How many songs have I sung?
How many more have I still to sing here on earth?
Within and without I have been searching for
  myself through my songs.
With deep pangs my heart cries;
My self-form is not visible yet.
In the vast life-ocean, I am floating all alone.

I LONG TO BE ONE

I long to be one
With the Dust of Your Feet.
I long to be one
With the Smile of Your Eyes.
I long to be one
With the Love of Your Heart.
I long to be one
With the Oars of Your Boat.
I long to be one
With the Glow of Your Promise.
I long to be one
With the Flow of Your Life.
I long to be one
With the Victory of Your Banner.

BE THOU

Be Thou
My hands,
That I can give.

Be Thou
My ears,
That I can receive.

Be Thou
My eyes,
That I can dream.

Be Thou
My heart,
That I can achieve.

APOCALYPSE

Within, without the cosmos wide am I;
In joyful sweep I loose forth and draw back all.
A birthless deathless Spirit that moves and is still
Ever abides within to hear my call.

I who create on earth my joys and doles
To fulfil my matchless quest in all my play,
I veil my face of truth with golden hues
And see the serpent-night and python-day.

A Consciousness-Bliss I feel in each breath;
I am the self-amorous child of the Sun.
At will I break and build my symbol sheath
And freely enjoy the world's unshadowed fun.

REVELATION

No more my heart shall sob or grieve.
My days and nights dissolve in God's own Light.
Above the toil of life, my soul
Is a Bird of Fire winging the Infinite.

I have known the One and His secret Play
And passed beyond the sea of Ignorance-Dream.
In tune with Him, I sport and sing;
I own the golden Eye of the Supreme.

Drunk deep of Immortality,
I am the root and boughs of a teeming vast.
My Form I have known and realised.
The Supreme and I are one; all we outlast.

FAREWELL TIME

It is farewell time.
The play of the heart will now begin.
The banner of divine Love will fly today
In the boundless sky.
The sun, the moon, the deathless Consciousness,
Infinity's secret wealth,
The World-Lord's very Feet,
Far Heaven's Blessing-Message,
The flood of liberation, the Abode of divine Nectar,
All will be united in the heart of our world.

MY LIFE'S LAST GAME

My time is passing away.
My time is passing away.
O, where are You,
    My life's last game?

FATHER-SON

O Supreme, my Father-Son,
Now that we two are one
And won by each other, won,
Nothing remains undone.

EVER THE SAME AGAIN

Ever the same again,
My lost Truth rediscovered.
Ever the same again.

Ever the same again,
My forgotten Self remembered.
Ever the same again.

Ever the same again,
My lost Goal regained.
Ever the same again.

THE ABSOLUTE

No mind, no form, I only exist;
   Now ceased all will and thought;
The final end of Nature's dance,
   I am It whom I have sought.

A realm of Bliss bare, ultimate;
   Beyond both knower and known;
A rest immense I enjoy at last;
   I face the One alone.

I have crossed the secret ways of life,
   I have become the Goal.
The Truth immutable is revealed;
   I am the way, the God-Soul.

My spirit aware of all the heights,
   I am mute in the core of the Sun.
I barter nothing with time and deeds;
   My cosmic play is done.

APPENDIX

Bibliography

p. 13. Sri Chinmoy, *My Flute*, Sri Chinmoy Lighthouse, New York, 1972.

p. 14. Sri Chinmoy, *My Flute*, Sri Chinmoy Lighthouse, New York, 1972.

p. 15. Sri Chinmoy, *My Flute,* Sri Chinmoy Lighthouse, New York, 1972.

p. 16. *My Flute,* Sri Chinmoy Lighthouse, New York, 1972.

p. 17. Sri Chinmoy, *AUM The Message of Sri Chinmoy — Vol. II-2, No. 6*, Vishma Press, 1975.

p. 18. Sri Chinmoy, *My Flute*, Sri Chinmoy Lighthouse, New York, 1972.

p. 19. Sri Chinmoy, *Illumination-Song and Liberation-Dance, part 5,* Agni Press, 1976.

p. 20. Sri Chinmoy, *Supreme, teach me how to cry,* 1975.

p. 21. Sri Chinmoy, *Patience-Groves*, Agni Press 1978.

p. 22. Sri Chinmoy, *Pole-Star Promise-Light, part 2*, 1977.

p. 23. Sri Chinmoy, *The seeker's universe*, Sri Chinmoy Centre, Jamaica, West Indies, 1971.

p. 24. Sri Chinmoy, *Supreme, teach me how to surrender,* 1975.

p. 25. Sri Chinmoy, *Garden of Love-Light, part 2,* 1973.

p. 26. Sri Chinmoy, *Pole-Star Promise-Light, part 2*, 1977.

p. 27. Sri Chinmoy, *Supreme, teach me how to surrender,* 1975.

p. 28. Sri Chinmoy, *The Dance of Life, part 2*, Aum Press, Puerto Rico, 1973.

p. 29. Sri Chinmoy, *The Dance of Life, part 1*, Aum Press, Puerto Rico, 1973.

p. 30. Sri Chinmoy, *The Wings of Light, part 7*, Aum Press, Puerto Rico, 1974.

p. 31. Sri Chinmoy, *The Dance of Life, part 5*, Aum Press, Puerto Rico, 1973.

p. 32. Sri Chinmoy, *The Dance of Life, part 1*, Aum Press, Puerto Rico, 1973.

p. 33. Sri Chinmoy, *The Dance of Life, part 13*, Aum Press, Puerto Rico, 1973.

p. 34. Sri Chinmoy, *Patience-Groves*, Agni Press, NY, 1978.

p. 35. Sri Chinmoy, *The Dance of Life, part 1*, Aum Press, Puerto Rico, 1973.

p. 36. Sri Chinmoy, *My Flute*, Sri Chinmoy Lighthouse, New York, 1972.

p. 37. Sri Chinmoy, *My Flute*, Sri Chinmoy Lighthouse, New York, 1972.

p. 38. Sri Chinmoy, *The Goal is Won*, Sri Chinmoy Centre, New York, 1974.

p. 39. Sri Chinmoy, *The Dance of Life, part 3*, Aum Press, Puerto Rico, 1973.

p. 40. Sri Chinmoy, *Supreme, teach me how to cry*, Agni Press, 1974.

p. 41. Sri Chinmoy, *The Wings of Light, part 12*, Aum Press, Puerto Rico, 1974.

p. 42. Sri Chinmoy, *Bela chale jai,* Agni Press 1979.

p. 43. Sri Chinmoy, *My Flute*, Sri Chinmoy Lighthouse, New York, 1972.

p. 44. Sri Chinmoy, *The Prayer of the Sky*, Agni Press, 1974.

p. 45. Sri Chinmoy, *Eternity's Silence-Heart*, Agni Press, 1974.

p. 46. Sri Chinmoy, *The Wings of Light, part 15*, Agni Press, 1974.

p. 47. Sri Chinmoy, *The Wings of Light, part 20*, Agni Press, 1974.

p. 48. Sri Chinmoy, *Patience-Groves*, Agni Press 1978.

p. 49. Sri Chinmoy, *Patience-Groves*, Agni Press 1978.

p. 50. Sri Chinmoy, *My Flute*, Sri Chinmoy Lighthouse, New York, 1972.

p. 51. Sri Chinmoy, *Pole-Star Promise-Light, part 2*, Agni Press, 1977.

p. 52. Sri Chinmoy, *My Flute*, Sri Chinmoy Lighthouse, New York, 1972.

p. 53. Sri Chinmoy, *Garden of Love-Light, part 2*, Aum Press, Puerto Rico, 1975.

p. 54. Sri Chinmoy, *The Dance of Life, part 1,* Aum Press, Puerto Rico, 1973.

p. 55. Sri Chinmoy, *The Dance of Life, part 15*, Aum Press, Puerto Rico, 1973.

p. 56. Sri Chinmoy, *My Flute*, Sri Chinmoy Lighthouse, New York, 1972.

p. 57. Sri Chinmoy, *My Flute*, Sri Chinmoy Lighthouse, New York, 1972.

p. 58. Sri Chinmoy, *Garden of Love-Light, part 1*, Aum Press, Puerto Rico, 1974.

p. 59. Sri Chinmoy, *Bela chale jai*, Agni Press 1979.

p. 60. Sri Chinmoy, *The seeker's universe*, Sri Chinmoy Centre, Jamaica, West Indies, 1971.

p. 61. Sri Chinmoy, *My Flute*, Sri Chinmoy Lighthouse, New York, 1972.

p. 62. Sri Chinmoy, *My Flute*, Sri Chinmoy Lighthouse, New York, 1972.

www.ingramcontent.com/pod-product-compliance
Lightning Source LLC
Chambersburg PA
CBHW030044100526
44590CB00011B/322